PRINCEWILL LAGANG

Love in Later Life: Navigating Retirement as a Couple

First published by PRINCEWILL LAGANG 2023

Copyright © 2023 by Princewill Lagang

All rights reserved. No part of this publication may be reproduced, stored or transmitted in any form or by any means, electronic, mechanical, photocopying, recording, scanning, or otherwise without written permission from the publisher. It is illegal to copy this book, post it to a website, or distribute it by any other means without permission.

Princewill Lagang asserts the moral right to be identified as the author of this work.

First edition

This book was professionally typeset on Reedsy. Find out more at reedsy.com

Contents

1	Introduction	1
2	The Transition to Retirement	3
3	Redefining Roles and Identities	6
4	Communicating Retirement Plans	9
5	Shared Hobbies and Activities	12
6	Balancing Togetherness and Independence	15
7	Financial Planning and Lifestyle Adjustments	18
8	Health and Wellness in Later Life	21
9	Navigating Empty Nest Syndrome	24
10	Intimacy and Connection in Later Life	27
11	Embracing Change and Adaptability	30
12	Reflection and Legacy	33

1

Introduction

In this opening chapter, we embark on a journey to uncover the intricate dynamics that surround the institution of marriage during the often uncharted territory of retirement. As couples transition from their professional lives into the realm of retirement, a new chapter of their relationship begins—one that is rife with both challenges and opportunities. In this book, we delve into the heart of these changes, aiming to shed light on the complex interplay of emotions, adjustments, and growth that unfold.

1.1 Exploring Marriage in Retirement

Our focus rests squarely on the concept of marriage during the retirement years. These years are marked by a shift in priorities, roles, and expectations, which can significantly impact the marital relationship. As couples move away from the structured routines of their working lives, they are confronted with a fresh set of circumstances that demand their attention, understanding, and adaptability. We aim to uncover the nuances of how these changes influence the nature of their relationship.

1.2 Navigating Unique Challenges

Retirement brings with it a series of unique challenges that can test even the strongest of unions. The sudden abundance of unstructured time, the potential loss of identity tied to a career, and the adjustments required when two individuals are suddenly together for extended periods can all strain the marital fabric. We will delve into these challenges, exploring ways couples can navigate them while maintaining a strong and healthy bond.

1.3 Embracing New Opportunities

However, it's not all trials and tribulations. Retirement also ushers in a wealth of opportunities for couples to rekindle their connection and embark on shared adventures. With the freedom to explore new hobbies, travel, and engage in activities they've long postponed, couples can forge deeper connections and create lasting memories. We will investigate how couples can seize these opportunities to reinforce their bond and foster personal growth.

1.4 The Structure of the Book

In the chapters that follow, we will journey through a comprehensive exploration of the facets that shape marriage during retirement. We will delve into communication strategies, emotional well-being, financial considerations, and the intricacies of shared decision-making. Through real-life anecdotes, expert insights, and research-based guidance, we hope to equip couples with the tools they need to not only weather the challenges of retirement but also thrive in this new chapter of their lives together.

As we embark on this enlightening expedition into the realm of marriage during retirement, let us remember that while the path may be uncertain, the insights we gain can illuminate the way forward for couples seeking to cultivate a resilient and fulfilling partnership in their golden years.

2

The Transition to Retirement

In this chapter, we embark on an exploration of the transformative journey that individuals undergo as they transition from the familiar rhythms of work life to the uncharted territory of retirement. This period of transition is marked by profound emotional and lifestyle changes that can significantly impact individuals and their relationships.

2.1 Farewell to Work Life

The shift from the structured routine of work life to the open canvas of retirement can be both liberating and unsettling. The daily rhythms tied to a career—commuting, meetings, deadlines—fade away, leaving individuals to define their own schedules. The departure from the workplace also brings a sense of loss, as one's professional identity and sense of purpose are redefined. We will explore the emotional intricacies of bidding farewell to a career and the implications this has on one's self-esteem and overall well-being.

2.2 Embracing New Routines

As the boundaries between work and leisure blur, retirees must create new routines that provide structure and purpose to their days. Finding meaning beyond a job title can be a challenge, but it also offers the freedom to engage in activities that were once relegated to the periphery. We will discuss strategies for establishing fulfilling routines that balance personal pursuits and shared activities with a partner.

2.3 The Emotional Landscape

Retirement often stirs a mix of emotions, ranging from excitement and anticipation to anxiety and uncertainty. The prospect of an abundance of leisure time can be thrilling, yet the loss of the familiar work environment can also trigger feelings of isolation and a sense of purposelessness. Couples may find themselves navigating these emotional landscapes together, requiring open communication and empathy. We will explore techniques for acknowledging and managing these emotions constructively.

2.4 Redefining Roles

The retirement transition prompts a renegotiation of roles within couples. Individuals who once defined themselves through their careers must now navigate new roles and responsibilities. This redefinition can lead to power dynamics and conflicts as partners strive to find their place in the post-work era. We will delve into the process of redefining roles, highlighting the importance of mutual understanding and compromise.

2.5 Embracing Change Together

As couples grapple with the transition to retirement, they are presented with a unique opportunity to deepen their bond. Sharing in the process of adapting to a new way of life can foster a sense of unity and mutual support. By embracing change together, couples can explore new horizons, create shared goals, and draw strength from each other's companionship. We will discuss strategies for nurturing this partnership in the face of change.

In the pages that follow, we will navigate the uncharted waters of the retirement transition, uncovering the emotions, challenges, and rewards that come with it. By understanding the emotional intricacies of this phase, individuals and couples can set the foundation for a fulfilling retirement journey, marked by growth, connection, and shared purpose.

3

Redefining Roles and Identities

In this chapter, we delve into the intricate process of redefining roles and identities that unfolds as individuals and couples transition from the world of work into retirement. The shifts in routines and responsibilities during this phase can trigger a reevaluation of self-identity and a reimagining of one's purpose.

3.1 The Evolving Self

Retirement often prompts individuals to ask themselves, "Who am I now?" The roles and titles that once defined them in the professional sphere may no longer apply. This departure from the career-driven identity can evoke feelings of uncertainty and even loss. We will examine the journey of self-discovery that individuals embark upon as they seek to reframe their identities beyond their professional accomplishments.

3.2 The Impact on Relationships

As individuals grapple with self-identity questions, these internal changes can have a profound impact on their relationships with their partners. The ways in which couples perceive each other, their strengths, and their contributions may shift. This can lead to either newfound appreciation or potential conflict as individuals navigate the recalibration of expectations. We will explore how couples can communicate openly to understand and support each other's evolving identities.

3.3 Navigating Role Changes

The traditional roles and responsibilities that partners assumed during their working years may require adjustment in retirement. One partner's shift from breadwinner to equal contributor can lead to feelings of empowerment or vulnerability. Couples must communicate effectively to redefine their roles in a way that respects individual strengths and desires. We will discuss strategies for fostering flexibility and balance in the distribution of tasks and responsibilities.

3.4 Finding Purpose

The search for purpose becomes paramount in retirement, as the absence of the daily work routine can leave a void in individuals' lives. This quest for meaning goes beyond hobbies and leisure activities—it involves identifying activities that provide a sense of fulfillment and contribute to personal growth. We will explore avenues for individuals to discover and pursue activities that align with their passions and values, enriching their sense of purpose.

3.5 Reinventing Together

While individual self-discovery is vital, the redefinition of roles and identities also presents an opportunity for couples to reimagine their relationship. By embracing change as a shared endeavor, couples can forge a deeper connection and build a relationship that continues to evolve with the changing seasons of life. We will provide guidance on how couples can collaborate to support each other's growth and aspirations.

As we journey through the process of redefining roles and identities, we'll uncover the potential for personal growth, increased self-awareness, and enhanced relationship dynamics. By embracing the fluidity of identity and fostering open communication, individuals and couples can navigate the transitions of retirement with grace and resilience.

4

Communicating Retirement Plans

In this chapter, we delve into the critical role of open and effective communication when it comes to retirement planning. As couples transition into retirement, aligning their expectations, discussing their goals, and crafting a shared vision for the future become essential for maintaining a harmonious and fulfilling partnership.

4.1 The Power of Dialogue

Retirement brings with it a series of decisions that impact both individuals and their relationships. Engaging in meaningful conversations about retirement plans can help partners uncover shared aspirations, uncover potential conflicts, and ensure that their dreams align. We will explore the ways in which honest and respectful communication can set the stage for a successful retirement journey.

4.2 Unearthing Individual Goals

Each partner may have unique desires and visions for their retirement. Whether it's traveling the world, dedicating time to hobbies, or investing in personal growth, these individual goals must be brought to the surface. By discussing these aspirations openly, couples can understand each other's motivations and work toward integrating their separate dreams into a unified plan.

4.3 Defining Shared Goals

In addition to individual goals, couples must collaborate to establish shared goals for their retirement. This includes considerations such as where to live, financial plans, healthcare decisions, and lifestyle preferences. Openly addressing these topics can prevent misunderstandings and ensure that both partners are on the same page when it comes to the future they envision.

4.4 Navigating Financial Discussions

Financial matters often take center stage during retirement planning discussions. Partners must address questions about savings, investments, budgeting, and potential income streams. These conversations can be complex and emotionally charged, but they are vital for setting realistic expectations and avoiding surprises down the road. We will discuss strategies for approaching financial conversations with transparency and sensitivity.

4.5 Crafting a Unified Vision

The ultimate goal of these discussions is to create a unified vision for retirement that reflects the desires and values of both partners. By weaving together individual aspirations and shared goals, couples can forge a roadmap that guides their decisions and actions. We will provide practical advice on how to merge personal and collective visions into a comprehensive plan.

4.6 Adapting and Reevaluating

Retirement planning is not a one-time conversation; it's an ongoing dialogue that requires flexibility and adaptation. As circumstances change and new opportunities arise, couples must be willing to reevaluate their plans and make adjustments as needed. By maintaining open lines of communication, couples can navigate unexpected changes with resilience and unity.

As we navigate the terrain of communicating retirement plans, we discover the power of shared dreams, open conversations, and mutual understanding. By embracing these principles, couples can embark on their retirement journey with clarity, confidence, and a strong sense of partnership.

5

Shared Hobbies and Activities

In this chapter, we explore the enriching role of shared interests and hobbies in the context of retirement. Engaging in activities together not only deepens the connection between couples but also offers a pathway to personal growth, mutual enjoyment, and a sense of purpose during this new phase of life.

5.1 The Bonds of Shared Activities

Participating in hobbies and activities as a couple can cultivate a sense of togetherness and camaraderie. These shared experiences create lasting memories and provide opportunities for meaningful interactions. We will discuss the importance of nurturing common interests to strengthen the bond between partners and foster a sense of unity.

5.2 Exploring New Horizons

Retirement provides a unique chance for couples to explore passions they may not have had time for during their working years. From taking up painting to learning a musical instrument, the possibilities are vast. Engaging in new activities not only adds excitement but also encourages personal growth and creativity. We will offer insights into discovering and embracing these uncharted territories.

5.3 Navigating Differences

While shared hobbies can be a source of connection, couples may still have differing interests. Balancing individual pursuits with joint activities requires open communication and a willingness to compromise. We will provide strategies for finding common ground while also respecting each other's individual passions.

5.4 Revitalizing Established Hobbies

Couples often enter retirement with hobbies they have enjoyed individually. Transitioning these activities into shared experiences can breathe new life into them. By approaching these pursuits collaboratively, partners can introduce fresh perspectives and revitalize their enjoyment. We will explore ways to transform individual hobbies into joint endeavors.

5.5 Cultivating a Sense of Purpose

Engaging in shared hobbies and activities can contribute to a sense of purpose in retirement. Pursuits that align with personal interests and values infuse daily life with meaning and fulfillment. As couples navigate this phase together, they can lean on these shared passions to anchor their sense of purpose and invigorate their spirits.

5.6 Ideas for Shared Activities

To inspire couples, we will provide a range of ideas for shared activities—ranging from physical pursuits like hiking and dancing to creative endeavors like cooking or writing. We'll also delve into the benefits of volunteering and community involvement as ways to not only connect with each other but also give back to the world around them.

As we delve into the world of shared hobbies and activities, we uncover the potential for joy, personal growth, and enhanced connection. By embracing both familiar passions and new pursuits, couples can embark on a retirement journey that is rich in experiences, shared aspirations, and a renewed zest for life together.

6

Balancing Togetherness and Independence

In this chapter, we delve into the delicate art of finding equilibrium between spending quality time together as a couple and nurturing individuality during retirement. Striking the right balance between togetherness and independence is crucial for maintaining a healthy, harmonious relationship in this new phase of life.

6.1 The Dynamics of Togetherness

Spending time together is a cornerstone of any relationship, and retirement provides ample opportunity for couples to do just that. Engaging in shared activities and pursuits can deepen the bond and foster shared experiences. We will explore the significance of togetherness while also highlighting the need to preserve individual space.

6.2 Nurturing Individuality

While togetherness is important, maintaining a sense of individuality is equally crucial. Each partner brings their own interests, passions, and need for personal space to the relationship. Embracing individuality can prevent feelings of suffocation and contribute to a more enriching partnership. We will discuss strategies for cultivating personal growth while in a committed relationship.

6.3 Communicating Boundaries

Open communication is essential when it comes to discussing boundaries and expectations regarding time spent together and apart. Partners must feel comfortable expressing their need for space and time alone without fear of damaging the relationship. We will explore the ways in which clear communication can lead to mutual understanding and respect.

6.4 Fostering Interests Apart

Retirement provides an excellent opportunity for individuals to immerse themselves in hobbies and interests that bring them joy. These pursuits not only enrich individual lives but also enhance the overall relationship by creating a sense of contentment and personal fulfillment. We will delve into strategies for nurturing these interests while also supporting each other's passions.

6.5 Shared Goals, Individual Journeys

In the pursuit of balance, couples can work together to define shared goals while allowing each partner to chart their individual path toward those goals. This approach acknowledges that each person's journey is unique, even when moving toward common aspirations. We will discuss the benefits of aligning shared goals with the freedom to pursue them in ways that resonate personally.

6.6 Practicing Mutual Respect

BALANCING TOGETHERNESS AND INDEPENDENCE

Respecting each other's need for independence and space is the cornerstone of a harmonious partnership during retirement. By honoring each other's boundaries and being understanding of different preferences, couples can foster an environment where both togetherness and individuality can flourish.

As we navigate the delicate dance of balancing togetherness and independence, we uncover the power of maintaining a strong sense of self while nurturing a thriving relationship. By recognizing the importance of both aspects and fostering open communication, couples can create a retirement journey that is characterized by both unity and personal growth.

7

Financial Planning and Lifestyle Adjustments

In this chapter, we delve into the critical realm of financial planning and the necessary lifestyle adjustments that come with retirement. From budgeting to managing retirement funds, striking a balance between financial stability and maintaining a fulfilling lifestyle becomes paramount for couples entering this new phase of life.

7.1 The Importance of Financial Planning

Retirement necessitates careful financial planning to ensure a secure and comfortable future. Couples must assess their sources of income, retirement savings, investments, and potential expenses. Understanding their financial landscape empowers them to make informed decisions and navigate the years ahead with confidence.

7.2 Budgeting for Retirement

Creating a comprehensive budget that aligns with retirement income is fundamental. Couples should factor in essentials like housing, healthcare, and daily living costs while leaving room for discretionary spending. We will explore strategies for crafting a balanced budget that reflects both partners' priorities and goals.

7.3 Managing Retirement Funds

Managing retirement funds requires a blend of caution and strategic thinking. Couples must decide how to draw from their savings and investments in a way that supports their lifestyle without depleting their resources too quickly. We will discuss methods for maintaining financial stability while also accounting for inflation and potential unexpected expenses.

7.4 Lifestyle Adjustments

Retirement often brings with it a change in lifestyle due to shifts in income and priorities. Couples may need to adjust their spending habits, find cost-effective alternatives, and let go of certain luxuries. Embracing these adjustments can lead to a more stress-free and enjoyable retirement experience. We will explore ways to navigate these shifts with grace.

7.5 Maintaining a Fulfilling Lifestyle

While financial adjustments are necessary, they need not detract from a fulfilling retirement lifestyle. Couples can discover creative ways to enjoy their newfound free time and pursue meaningful experiences without breaking the bank. We will provide ideas for enjoying hobbies, travel, and leisure activities that align with their budget.

7.6 Continual Evaluation

Financial planning is not a one-time task; it requires ongoing evaluation and adjustment. As circumstances change and retirement unfolds, couples should periodically reassess their financial strategy to ensure it remains aligned with their goals and aspirations. We will discuss the benefits of regularly reviewing and adapting their financial plan.

Navigating the intersection of financial planning and lifestyle adjustments during retirement demands careful consideration and proactive management. By embracing a well-thought-out financial strategy and making thoughtful lifestyle choices, couples can embark on their retirement journey with the assurance of financial security and the opportunity for a rewarding and fulfilling lifestyle.

8

Health and Wellness in Later Life

In this chapter, we explore the critical dimension of health and wellness as individuals and couples navigate the realm of retirement. Maintaining physical and mental well-being becomes pivotal for a fulfilling and vibrant life during this phase.

8.1 The Significance of Well-Being

As couples transition into retirement, prioritizing health and wellness becomes paramount. A robust physical and mental state enhances the quality of life, enabling individuals to fully enjoy the opportunities that retirement offers. We will discuss how well-being forms the foundation for a vibrant and enriching retirement journey.

8.2 Staying Physically Active

Engaging in regular physical activity is a cornerstone of health in later life. Couples can embark on joint activities like walking, cycling, or dancing to stay active together. Exercise not only contributes to physical fitness but also fosters emotional well-being and offers opportunities for shared experiences.

8.3 Nurturing Mental Wellness

Retirement brings changes that can impact mental health, including feelings of purposelessness or isolation. Engaging in intellectual pursuits, learning new skills, and staying socially connected are essential strategies for nurturing mental wellness. We will discuss the importance of staying mentally engaged and how couples can support each other in this endeavor.

8.4 Prioritizing Preventive Health Measures

Regular health check-ups, screenings, and preventive measures are essential for individuals entering their later years. Partners can encourage and accompany each other to medical appointments, ensuring that health concerns are identified and addressed promptly. We will explore ways to prioritize preventive health care as a couple.

8.5 Supporting Each Other's Wellness

As couples navigate health and wellness in retirement, mutual support becomes crucial. Partners can act as accountability buddies, encouraging each other to make healthy choices, engage in physical activity, and manage stress effectively. By fostering a culture of wellness, couples can navigate the challenges of aging together.

8.6 Embracing Holistic Wellness

Well-being encompasses more than just physical and mental health—it extends to emotional, spiritual, and social aspects of life. Couples can explore practices like mindfulness, meditation, and fostering meaningful connections with others. We will discuss the holistic approach to wellness and its benefits during retirement.

8.7 Adapting to Changing Health Needs

As retirement progresses, health needs may change. Couples must be prepared to adapt their routines, activities, and even living arrangements to accommodate evolving health requirements. We will explore strategies for addressing these changes with flexibility and grace.

By prioritizing health and wellness during retirement, couples can set the stage for a vibrant, enriching, and meaningful life together. Through shared activities, open communication, and mutual support, individuals can embrace the journey of aging with resilience and a sense of fulfillment.

9

Navigating Empty Nest Syndrome

In this chapter, we delve into the complexities of the empty nest syndrome during retirement, a phase that brings both challenges and opportunities. As children leave the family home, couples experience a significant shift in their dynamics, requiring them to reevaluate their relationship and create a renewed sense of partnership.

9.1 The Transition to an Empty Nest

The departure of children from the family home marks a significant life transition. While this phase can trigger feelings of loss and adjustment, it also opens the door to new possibilities and a reimagining of the couple's relationship. We will discuss the emotional landscape of empty nest syndrome during retirement.

9.2 Rediscovering Each Other

With children gone, couples have the opportunity to focus on their relationship in a new way. This phase allows partners to rediscover each other's interests, dreams, and aspirations, fostering a deeper connection. We will explore strategies for nurturing this renewed sense of partnership.

9.3 Pursuing Personal Goals

As couples navigate the empty nest phase, they can turn their attention to personal goals and interests that may have been put on hold during their child-rearing years. This period offers the freedom to explore new passions and reinvent individual identities. We will discuss the importance of supporting each other's individual pursuits.

9.4 Communication and Reconnection

Open communication is paramount as couples navigate the empty nest phase. Honest conversations about expectations, plans, and shared aspirations can lead to a more harmonious partnership. We will delve into the ways in which couples can effectively communicate and reconnect during this transformative phase.

9.5 Fostering Shared Experiences

While the empty nest phase encourages individual growth, couples should also make deliberate efforts to create shared experiences. Travel, hobbies, and joint projects can infuse the relationship with a sense of adventure and unity. We will discuss the benefits of actively fostering shared moments.

9.6 Cultivating a New Chapter

Empty nest syndrome during retirement is an opportunity for couples to cultivate a new chapter of their lives together. By embracing change, communicating openly, and supporting each other's growth, partners can navigate this phase with resilience and create a relationship that continues to evolve and thrive.

As we explore the complexities of navigating the empty nest syndrome during retirement, we uncover the potential for personal growth, renewed connection, and a sense of purpose. By approaching this phase with intention and openness, couples can embark on a journey that strengthens their bond and paves the way for a fulfilling future together.

10

Intimacy and Connection in Later Life

In this chapter, we delve into the essential aspects of emotional and physical intimacy during the retirement phase. Nurturing a deep sense of connection and maintaining a vibrant spark in the relationship becomes pivotal for couples entering this new chapter of their lives.

10.1 The Essence of Intimacy

Intimacy encompasses emotional closeness, trust, and a shared vulnerability. In retirement, as couples navigate new dynamics and opportunities, fostering and preserving intimacy takes on heightened significance. We will discuss the importance of intimacy as a cornerstone of a thriving relationship.

10.2 Navigating Changing Dynamics

As individuals and couples transition into retirement, the dynamics of their relationship may shift. It's crucial to address these changes openly and honestly, recognizing that they may impact intimacy. Partners must be attuned to each other's emotional needs and work together to maintain a strong connection.

10.3 Emotional Intimacy

Emotional intimacy involves deep conversations, active listening, and a willingness to share thoughts and feelings. During retirement, couples have more time to engage in these meaningful interactions, which can strengthen their emotional bond and foster mutual understanding. We will discuss strategies for cultivating emotional intimacy.

10.4 Physical Intimacy

Physical intimacy remains a vital component of a romantic relationship during retirement. As couples age, physical changes may occur, requiring open communication and adaptability. Couples can explore ways to prioritize physical connection and intimacy in ways that are comfortable and satisfying for both partners.

10.5 Keeping the Spark Alive

Maintaining the spark in a long-term relationship demands effort and creativity. Couples can explore new ways to surprise each other, plan romantic outings, and prioritize shared moments. We will provide ideas for kindling the romance and keeping the relationship exciting and vibrant.

10.6 Mutual Exploration

Retirement presents an ideal opportunity for couples to embark on new adventures together, both emotionally and physically. Engaging in novel experiences, whether it's trying a new hobby or taking a spontaneous trip, can infuse the relationship with a sense of excitement and rekindle the sense of adventure.

10.7 Communication as a Catalyst

Open communication is the linchpin of intimacy. Couples must discuss their desires, preferences, and any concerns related to intimacy. By maintaining a dialogue that is free from judgment and imbued with understanding, partners can navigate the intricacies of intimacy with ease.

As we delve into the realms of emotional and physical intimacy during retirement, we uncover the potential for a relationship that thrives on connection, vulnerability, and mutual exploration. By valuing each other's emotional well-being and actively nurturing physical closeness, couples can embark on a retirement journey that is not only rich in shared experiences but also deeply fulfilling on a personal and intimate level.

11

Embracing Change and Adaptability

In this chapter, we explore the theme of change as an inevitable part of both later life and relationships. Navigating retirement requires couples to cultivate adaptability and resilience as they encounter shifts in roles, routines, and dynamics.

11.1 The Nature of Change

Change is a constant companion on the journey of life, and retirement is no exception. Partners must recognize that as they enter this new phase, their relationship will naturally evolve. Acknowledging the inevitability of change can lead to a proactive approach that embraces growth and transformation.

11.2 Navigating Role Transitions

Retirement often requires partners to redefine their roles within the relationship. The shift from work to leisure can alter power dynamics, responsibilities, and even self-identities. Couples must be open to renegotiating roles and responsibilities in a way that reflects their evolving desires and circumstances.

11.3 Embracing Flexibility

Flexibility is a hallmark of adaptability. Couples should approach retirement with an open mind, prepared to adjust plans and expectations as new opportunities and challenges arise. Embracing flexibility allows partners to navigate unexpected changes with resilience and a willingness to find solutions together.

11.4 Communicating Through Change

Effective communication is paramount when navigating change. Couples must feel comfortable discussing their feelings, concerns, and aspirations openly. Regular check-ins and heartfelt conversations can foster an environment where both partners are aligned in their approach to the evolving nature of retirement.

11.5 Cultivating Resilience

Resilience is the ability to bounce back from challenges and setbacks. Partners can cultivate resilience by fostering a positive mindset, seeking support when needed, and focusing on strengths rather than limitations. We will explore strategies for building resilience that can be applied to both individual growth and relationship dynamics.

11.6 Embracing New Beginnings

Change brings with it the potential for new beginnings. Partners can view retirement as an opportunity to embark on fresh journeys, individually and as a couple. By embracing the unknown with a sense of excitement and curiosity, couples can navigate change as an adventure that leads to personal and relational growth.

11.7 The Ever-Evolving Relationship

Couples must understand that their relationship will continue to evolve throughout retirement and beyond. Embracing this evolution as a natural part of life can foster a sense of acceptance and curiosity. The willingness to adapt and grow together can lead to a partnership that remains vibrant and fulfilling.

As we explore the theme of embracing change and adaptability, we uncover the potential for personal growth, shared experiences, and a resilient partnership. By approaching change with an open heart and a willingness to adapt, couples can navigate the complexities of retirement with grace, creating a relationship that thrives in the face of evolving circumstances.

12

Reflection and Legacy

In this final chapter, we embark on a journey of reflection and introspection, examining the evolution of love and partnership throughout the retirement years. We'll summarize the key takeaways from this book and offer guidance on how to create a deeply fulfilling and meaningful retirement together.

12.1 Reflecting on the Journey

As couples look back on their retirement journey, they may find that it was a tapestry woven with moments of joy, challenges, growth, and transformation. Reflection allows partners to celebrate their accomplishments, acknowledge the hurdles they've overcome, and appreciate the wisdom gained along the way.

12.2 Key Takeaways

Throughout this book, we've explored the various facets of marriage during retirement, from navigating transitions and fostering communication to nurturing intimacy and embracing change. Key takeaways include the significance of:

- Open communication to navigate challenges and share aspirations.
   - Balancing togetherness and independence to foster a harmonious relationship.
   - Prioritizing health, wellness, and shared activities for a fulfilling retirement lifestyle.
   - Nurturing intimacy and connection to strengthen the bond between partners.
   - Embracing change and adaptability as an opportunity for personal and relational growth.

12.3 Crafting a Fulfilling Legacy

Retirement is a phase where couples have the opportunity to reflect on the legacy they want to leave behind. Legacy extends beyond material possessions—it encompasses the impact individuals and couples make on each other's lives and on the world around them. Creating a fulfilling legacy involves living authentically, embracing their passions, and contributing positively to their community.

12.4 Finding Meaning and Purpose

As couples approach their later years, the search for meaning and purpose deepens. By reflecting on their values, aspirations, and experiences, couples can align their actions with their beliefs. Engaging in acts of kindness, volunteering, and nurturing relationships can infuse life with a sense of purpose that extends well beyond retirement.

12.5 Continual Growth and Exploration

Retirement does not mark the end of personal growth or adventure. Couples can continue to learn, explore, and challenge themselves in various ways. Whether through continued education, pursuing new hobbies, or embarking on new journeys, the retirement years offer a canvas for ongoing self-discovery.

12.6 Gratitude and Celebration

Ultimately, the retirement journey is a gift that couples can celebrate together. By expressing gratitude for the experiences they've shared, the challenges they've overcome, and the love that has blossomed over the years, partners can infuse their relationship with a sense of joy and contentment.

In closing, the retirement years are an opportunity for couples to write the final chapters of their love story with intention, gratitude, and a commitment to growth. By embracing the principles explored in this book, couples can create a retirement journey that is marked by resilience, mutual support, shared experiences, and a legacy of love that extends far beyond their years together.

Conclusion: Love and Fulfillment in Later Life

As we come to the end of this journey, we're reminded that love knows no age limits and that the retirement years are brimming with possibilities for growth, connection, and adventure. Throughout this book, we've explored the intricate dynamics of marriage during retirement, delving into the challenges, joys, and transformative moments that couples encounter as they navigate this new phase together.

In the realm of love, age is but a number. The pages of this book have illuminated the notion that love can not only survive but thrive in later life. The retirement years are not a time of winding down, but rather an opportunity to wind up the passions, pursuits, and closeness that define a thriving relationship.

Embracing retirement as a journey of growth allows couples to cultivate deeper connections, rekindle the spark of intimacy, and embark on new adventures hand in hand. It's a time to learn, unlearn, explore, and discover—both within ourselves and within the partnership we've built over the years.

As you stand at the threshold of this new chapter, we encourage you to approach retirement with an open heart, a curious spirit, and a commitment to nurturing your relationship. Remember that communication, respect, and shared experiences are the pillars that uphold a resilient and flourishing partnership.

The pages of this book have woven a narrative of hope, resilience, and the infinite possibilities that await as you step into the realm of retirement together. It's a journey that invites you to reflect on your journey so far, celebrate the moments you've shared, and create a legacy that's defined by love, authenticity, and purpose.

So, go forth with enthusiasm and confidence, for your journey of love is far from over. Let the retirement years be a canvas upon which you paint vibrant memories, write new stories, and inspire those around you with the beauty of a partnership that has weathered the seasons of life and emerged stronger, more united, and ever more in love.

www.ingramcontent.com/pod-product-compliance
Lightning Source LLC
LaVergne TN
LVHW010440070526
838199LV00066B/6111